MENDIP RAMBLES

Cover: Waldegrave Pool, Priddy (courtesy: Geoffrey Wright)

Frontispiece overleaf: Map showing main locations in and around Mendip, as well as points visited on the rambles. Starting points are shown in bold.

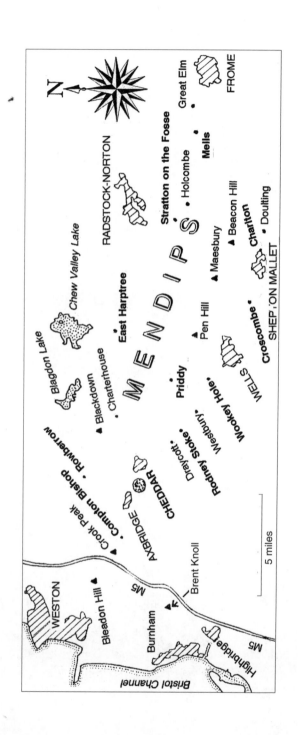

MENDIP RAMBLES

12 Best Walks on Mendip

Peter Wright

Illustrations by Julia Manning

EX LIBRIS PRESS

First edition 1985
Revised edition 1989
This edition 1997

EX LIBRIS PRESS
1 The Shambles
Bradford on Avon
Wiltshire

Typeset in 11 point Palatino and Briem Script

Design and typesetting by Ex Libris Press

.

Cover printed by Shires Press, Trowbridge
Printed and bound by
Cromwell Press, Broughton Gifford, Wiltshire

ISBN 0 948578 33 5

*For Alison and Jamie with so much love,
and Andrew and Carole for their encouragement*

CONTENTS

About the Author

The author, Peter Wright, was born in Bath in 1951 and writes about himself as follows: 'Occasionally attended Grammar School in Bradford on Avon, otherwise spent time climbing, bird-watching, and generally learning about the countryside. After school moved to Wensleydale, initially working in forestry, later self-employed at walling, fencing and all kinds of work on the fringes of agriculture; continued climbing. Moved to North Scotland in 1975 to work as a shepherd and resuscitator of moribund highland estate for two years. Spent several years based on sheep shearing in summer, working on any available jobs that could be combined with travelling for the rest of the year. Is now semi-domesticated with wife and young son working with stone in Somerset.'
Peter Wright moved back to North Scotland in 1985 – *Editor*

PREFACE

It was an absorbing pleasure recently to retrace these walks in the cause of revision and accuracy. I was relieved not to find scores of readers wandering dazedly about, footsore Flying Dutchmen, doomed to ramble the same path forever because a change had occurred. There is indeed evidence that the less obvious routes are now quite frequently used, which pleases me much. Any enthusiast likes others to experience what he has enjoyed. Such an unknown and surprising country lies behind the hedge, our secret land.

It was a good discipline for me to have to puzzle out the pathways, one has to observe the proprieties in exhorting people to ramble about; I confess I have a rather cavalier attitude to trespass, it's such fun, but one should not advocate it! In England, we are so instilled with the concept of the sanctity of private property, and the terrors of abusing it, it's an interesting social phenomenon; does it spring from the time of the Enclosures, and the landed gentry, particularly those who preserved game with such vigour and violence? There is no doubt that the two animals which have most significantly affected the countryside in the past were sheep, which were the direct cause of the destruction of many thousands of English villages, mostly in Tudor times; and pheasants, for whose 'protection' the woodlands were effectively closed. The country-dwellers watched, and an unease at being off the highway grew in the English conscience and is there still.

I was greatly saddened to find that the old village site at Holcombe has been ploughed out, so no more can you clearly see the evidence of its existence. No doubt aerial photographs will still reveal its presence, but for we earthbound wayfarers, that tangible link with our past has been obliterated. This sort of destruction is all too common; sometimes it makes news, when yet another office block or superstore is plonked over an historic site, and the archaeologists are given a few days to do a frenzied survey before the money-crazed developers lay their concrete and build another temple to Profit. More usually, Progress and Profit demand (they never ask) that some superficially insignificant feature – a barrow, a field pond, a lost village, be levelled to provide a few pounds more to help pay off the overdraft, and nothing is heard.

Why should we be concerned? The authorities let us visit castles and abbeys, Roman walls and forts and Stonehenge, and we may there be supplied with information and displays. These are our heritage. Wonderful, but far more important and evocative are the odd corners you find yourself, the overgrown ruins, standing stones, curious hummocks in hidden places – the remnants of old England which you have found and are thereby a personal experience, full of meaning, albeit obscure; you want no information leaflet, like a school child doing a project, you only require imagination. As it is now, any emotional experience at Stonehenge must be virtually impossible; but deep in the quiet countryside, some insignificant and secretive relic can rock you. The loss of any of these places diminishes us, for they are our folk memory; not the pageant and pomp of power, but the handiwork of the common man, you and me.

Mendip is fortunate in that it will probably never be so glamorous and advertised that it will suffer the raddled fate of parts of the Lake District or Snowdonia – 'each man kills the thing he loves' in action. It should always be possible to immerse oneself satisfactorily in rural peace on Mendip, with a riot of wild flowers in season; certainly some small changes will occur, but by and large the areas will stay yours for the experiencing.

Peter Wright

INTRODUCTION

As in building a house, when you start at the bottom and work up, so in considering an area. Most of the character, landscape and history of a region is directly related to the underlying rocks; even a shallow understanding adds an extra dimension to your enjoyment and appreciation.

Like so many hill areas in England, the Mendips have a fairly abrupt, definitive escarpment on one side, and the other edge is a more bedraggled affair, breaking up into valleys as it gradually loses height. Thus, the south-western face of Mendip gives us no problem in definition; from above Shepton Mallet the scarp becomes more assertive as it stands above Wells, then strides on north-west, rent by the great ravine of Cheddar Gorge, thence swinging westwards in a series of more isolated hills to tail away into the muddy Bristol Channel at Brean Down. The northern border is undeniable from the rocky ramparts of Dolebury above Churchill, by Burrington with its lovely Combe; as you travel by Blagdon to Chewton Mendip, the hills lie large above you. I now assume a rather arbitrary border by Radstock to Frome, and back west to Shepton Mallet by the A361, not for reasons of altitude but geology; the common factor being Mountain Limestone. This grey, hard, soluble stone is almost always associated with high ground, few streams, few trees, much mineral wealth. On Mendip, it is a thick crust, greatly warped and cracked, over a core of Old Red Sandstone. This sandstone appears through the top of the eroded arch of limestone to form the four highest points of Mendip; on Blackdown it makes its presence felt most with an area of peat and heather; it also forms Pen Hill, North Hill by Priddy, and Beacon Hill over which the Fosse Way climbs.

From extensive exploration of Mendip, I can safely say that nowhere will you find the Mountain Limestone strata laid level, as in the case in the Pennines; perhaps this is why there is no area of limestone pavement on Mendip. Some splendid effects arise from these steeply angled rocks, the most notable being Cheddar Gorge of course, where the dip of the strata makes one side sloping, the other extremely precipitous. Another remarkable instance may be seen in the quarries of Tedbury Camp, Vallis Vale and Egford, between Mells and Frome, where the almost vertical Mountain Limestone has been planed off level, and the much younger oolitic limestone lies horizontally upon it.

The gigantic earth movements have caused great complexities, sometimes heaving older rocks above younger – this is how the sandstone shows above Pen Hill – in places completely inverting the layers; and particularly in the coal field area, creating such a dog's breakfast of the seams that the coal field is no longer worked. All the churning about did, however, allow mineral-rich gases to burp forth from below, to be deposited in cracks and later to be discovered in the form of ore by chaps seeking lead and zinc.

Only one of the rambles described in this book impinges on the coal mining area, though for anyone interested in industrial archaeology, puzzling out intricate footpaths, or following old canals and railways it is paradise. There is a very local area of calamine workings around Shipham, the ore being a zinc compound finding a nearby market among the brass founders of Bristol. This mining is now defunct. The most interesting remains of mining on Mendip are those concerned with lead. You will often see 'gruffy ground' (from the same root word as 'grave'): areas of small opencast diggings.

There is some evidence that lead was worked on Mendip in prehistoric times, as the Romans seem to have quickly become active miners; a 'pig' of lead having been discovered which dates from only six years after Claudius invaded in AD

43. Leaden objects have been found in the lake villages below Mendip, which were certainly pre-Roman. While the principal mining settlement of the Roman period was undoubtedly at Charterhouse, another was discovered in the fifties near St. Cuthbert's at Priddy. The trade must have been considerable to justify the road that goes by Beacon Hill towards the high ridges of South Wiltshire, whence a choice could be made to go to Poole, or via Salisbury to the Solent. I'm sure it wasn't built for holidaymakers to the south coast.

Historically, there is a gap during the Dark Ages and it is not until 1189 that Mendip lead reappears in documents pertaining to the right of the See of Bath to dig for lead, not only to exploit a valuable resource financially, something the church has been ever skilled at, but practically; there was a great epoch of church-building, and churches need roofs, flashing, gutters, font-linings and so on.

From then on, the Mendips were perennially busy – many accounts occur of the methods of mining, the disputes, the chicanery – human nature was ever so. All this activity had an inevitable result – the veins became worked out, necessitating the digging of deeper shafts which, even with the use of gunpowder in the 1680s, was difficult, dangerous and increased flooding. The death-blow was struck in 1825 when the relaxation of import tax occurred, Spanish lead became competitive, and by the 1850s the industry was moribund. A few re-smelting enterprises blossomed briefly, as mentioned in the Priddy chapter, but the cause was lost. Now we can only treasure the relics, notably around Charterhouse, where there is as fine an array of 'buddles' or washing-pits as you will see in the land. An aerial photograph reveals the great complexity of this area.

There are other industrial relics of note on Mendip, almost all connected with water, and thus, scattered round the periphery of the high ground. Directly descending from the hills came wool. Sheep farming was the principal form of agriculture on the Mendips until the Enclosures, no doubt having been brought to a fairly high and profitable standard by the monks of the Middle Ages, a common theme throughout the country. Most Abbeys and the fine churches of England owe their grandeur to profits from wool, this area being no exception. The Carthusian monks set up a small community, whose site is now lost, at Charterhouse, and it's a good bet that they had a profound effect on the husbandry practices of the time.

In itself, wool is bulky, and greater profit as well as easier transport lies in its conversion to cloth, or knitwear. For some reason, the woven goods were mostly made in the eastern quarter – Mells, Frome and Nunney for example – while the Shepton Mallet and Wells fringe heard the clack of needles as stockings in particular were produced. Much of the work was done by outworkers, and as the industry declines, some silk-working was introduced. There were mills for grinding corn, of course, and very notably, papermills were founded, at Wookey Hole principally, making good use of clean, iron-free water.

The most noticeable industry on the Mendips is quarrying – in your rambling about, you will encounter tiny quarries for walling stone, slightly larger enterprises extracting freestone around Doulting, and vast, mechanised rents in the landscape, the roadstone quarries with their concomitant dust, noise, traffic and blasting. Working quarries are awful, but withal interesting in what they reveal; disused quarries are fascinating for the amateur geologist and naturalist; as a youth I spent many happy days learning to climb on these quiet rock faces.

Essentially, Mendip is still agricultural, and apart from some local hotspots, very quiet. You may have to share Charterhouse, Black Down or the slopes of Cheddar with numbers of people but on many of the walks you are more likely to be seen as an eccentric rarity. Being almost a marginal-land area, the Mendips have not suffered too much from the machinations of the agri-businessman, with his obsession in obliterating everything that stands in the way of making huge featureless expanses for the great god Barley. A few hedges and walls have gone, but there is still plenty of livestock to be seen, both dairy and beef cattle, and sheep, and so long as there are animals, there must be enclosures.

It is very interesting to compare the qualities of farms and farmers as you ramble about; as one who has erected many scores of miles of fencing, I feel competent to comment that most of the fencing is dreadful – prodigal use of barbed wire stapled to trees is not good – and the occasional farm where there is neat, taut wire, crossed by workmanlike stiles is a real treat. Little things – a well-laid hedge, a neatly stoned area around a cattle trough for example – speak volumes about the farming before you even consider the stock or crops.

Now and then you will find that your way lies across a ploughed field or through a standing crop. I'm a firm advocate that courtesy and consideration is due to the farmers, most of whom are human, and if you walk round a field you will help a little to create a better feeling between farmers and walkers. It is amazing how much damage a few size tens can cause, particularly in grass to be mown for hay or silage, and after all, you are a walker, so what matter a few yards extra round the edge? It is also surprising how often you find little problems which you can solve, and feel really good about it.

I remember once finding a sheep that didn't run off; on inspection, she had her horn caught under a tree-root and would most certainly have died soon had I not released her. If ever you see a sheep laid on her back, act, it is very common, notably in late spring; any farmer will be delighted that you right her, they soon die on their backs. Sheep caught in wire, hedges, briars; lambs down holes; cows and calves in ditches, I've met them all, and it adds to the interest of the day to keep your eye lifted for the unusual.

As I walk about, I like to be able to go home having seen something new or interesting, be it a bird or animal, flower or tree; often the most instructive time is when you sit under a tree and munch your lunch; the birds and beasties get on with their lives when you sit still. On Mendip there are plenty of foxes, deer and other wildlife, and you stand a good chance of encountering them as you walk unobtrusively along. There is also a large population of badgers, which you are less likely to see, but the discovery of badger's setts can become an addiction.

For the historically minded, Mendip has great riches; the cave homes of prehistoric men, at Cheddar, Wookey Hole, Burrington Combe and several other sites; the more obvious hillforts at Dolebury, Maesbury, Wadbury and Tedbury: all are of interest. There are innumerable barrows and earthworks, concentrated around Priddy, and a lot of Roman interest, though this is mostly to do with roads, the township at Charterhouse being very subdued remains, and the lead-mining activity being covered by later workings. The Dark Ages have left almost no trace on Mendip itself, though on the periphery of the area we find Saxon influence in the churches at Cheddar and Chewton Mendip, and there was a mint at Axbridge, and a small fort.

The Middle Ages have more to show for themselves. The great churches and abbeys are not on Mendip itself, though Mendip will have had its place in their economy; the only monastic settlement being founded at Charterhouse in the reign of Henry III. There are a few deserted medieval settlements, the clearest example being by Holcombe church. There are many churches worth a second look, most of them around the fringes of the hills.

What the Mendips tend to lack in wild, unfettered walking country, they more than compensate for in close-range interest. I strongly recommend that you acquire the excellent Ordnance Survey 1:25,000 (two and a half inches to the mile) Explorer maps listed later; they have a mass of detail, and the great advantage is that walls and hedges are marked. This is a great boon when your are trying to puzzle out the often very intricate and elusive tracks of the area. All the footpaths in this book have been checked for authenticity, and all are practicable; at a couple of points I have suggested minor diversions to overcome an impossible place.

It is apparent that some of the paths particularly in the south and east have been rarely trodden, which adds to the interest, but here especially you will find that shorts, or your slinky evening gown have drawbacks as, intrepid to the core you face barbed wire, chin-high nettles, jungles of briar and thorn, all the luxuriant Somerset growth of summer. The problems of jungle are less in winter – then your foe is mud, and your energy output is twice that of summer. I hope you are not put off by this, you will find great pleasure exploring the odd corners, and get closer to the countryside this way.

By the same token, good boots are advisable in all but a drought. You could wear wellies, but that makes a toil of a pleasure, and years of experience have persuaded me that wet feet are preferable. I always take some dry socks and shoes in the car to change into. Some light repast is a good idea too– it can be disturbingly bitter at 1,000 feet in wind and rain, and it is wisdom to keep the inner fires stoked.

Here, then, is Mendip; I wish you interesting and happy rambling in this absorbing area.

Peter Wright

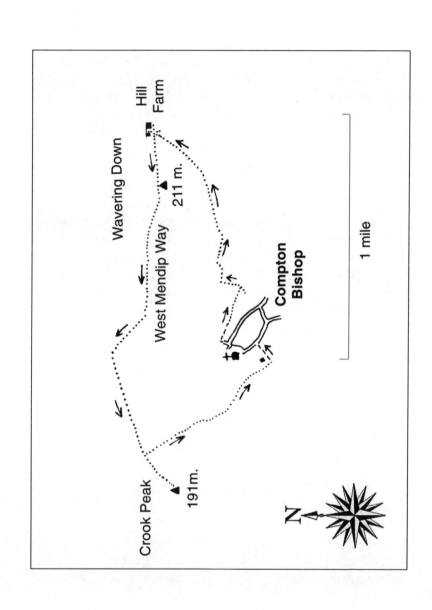

Hill Farm

Wavering Down

211 m.

West Mendip Way

Compton Bishop

Crook Peak

191m.

1 mile

N

1
COMPTON BISHOP
via Wavering Down and Crook Peak

From the quiet backwater village of Compton Bishop, this walk climbs gently on to the splendid ridge of Wavering Down, a walker's delight with its short dry turf, wide views and wildlife – would there were more of this on Mendip! There is an elegant col, a final short climb to the worthy vantage point of Crook Peak, after the mast of Pen Hill perhaps the best known landmark on Mendip to be seen from afar, then an easy, pleasant descent returns you to the village.

Start:	Compton Bishop
Map Reference:	396 554
Distance:	4 miles
Maps:	O.S. Explorer 4

Compton Bishop lies a mile north of the A38, just off the road from Axbridge to Loxton. There should be no problem parking somewhere near the church, remembering this is a farming village, and farm machinery needs room.

From the church, take Church Lane downhill, and ascend the lane opposite, beside a row of cypresses. Turn right with it, and go through the gate ahead, across a small stable yard, and across the foot of the next field to another gate. Follow the foot of the next field to an imperfect stile in the corner, and again make your way along the bottom of the field.

Here is a fine example of soil erosion; the ground you are treading is well above the original foot of the hedge, while the top headland of the field below is a good three feet below the original level, making a difference in level of at least five feet. It is an object lesson in the value of hedges, and a reminder of how much the land changes shape subtly.

Some way along this field, a track joins from the field below; at this point, you cease following the field boundary, instead climbing directly upwards to a high wall, below a shallow gully. When you reach the wall, cross the stile in the corner. Work your way uphill and right , presently climbing to clear yourself of the scrog of thorny woodland and gorse bushes. Your objective now is to continue slantwise up the slope to a point some 50 yards uphill to a thicket of yews you will see on the horizon. There are many sheep tracks on this hillside, and it is a matter of using the most hopeful.

Once above the yew thicket, Axbridge reservoir comes into view, two and a half miles distant on your right; your way contours round the hill to Hill Farm which soon becomes visible. At Hill Farm, a glorious site but windy I imagine, you join the West Mendip Way, turn left, up the hill, the path from here on being wide and unmistakeable, climbing beside a drystone wall amply decorated with barbed wire.

This also marks the new-fangled county boundary between Somerset and Avon. However, one of the joys of being on the hills is that the things of everyday, humdrum life, the less congenial aspects of the modern world diminish to their true insignificance; so as your stride along this fine hill-top, be blithe that whatever bureaucracy says, the land to your right is as surely Somerset as the fine view to your left. That is a splendid panorama of hills near and far, of bright rhines and rivers, the battleship bulk of Brean Down jutting defiance at the distant bulk of Wales. Up here, above the world and below the larks, is a great place to pass some hours putting things into perspective.

> Having once more girded the loins, keep walking west, soon dropping some 150 feet to a graceful col, still following the wall until it turns right. Now you attack the slope ahead, a brief burst of energy delivers you to the top of Crook Peak, its crooked crest being a small limestone outcrop.

Here is another excellent viewpoint, more than 600 feet above the grey levels of the Bristol Channel, some 180 metres proud of the M5 – which is perhaps as proud as one could be of the M5. Here is relativity in action – those on the motorway feel to be travelling so fast, yet how tardy they appear from your vantage, a mere centipede-speed.

> Now the climbing is done, it's downhill all the way, first of all returning to the bend in the wall whence you came. Take the track down to the right, roughly heading for a white house in the distance. The track descends through thorn scrub with an occasional elder and ash, a good place for birds. As the path passes above fields, the woodland thickens – after passing above a big house, take a sharp left, down a narrow lane leading onto Butts' Batch. Turn left, past an attractive farm back to the church.

This church is that happy rarity, one that is often open. Within is a fine carved pulpit, though marred by the later addition by a less creditable sculptor. There is a sturdy Norman font, surmounted by a wildly ornate cover, and some interesting stained glass. Outside is an unusual cross. It is, I find, quite easy to cast the imagination back a few centuries – nothing much has changed in this quiet nook in the hills.

Above: Compton Bishop, Walk 1; Below: Map for Walk 2

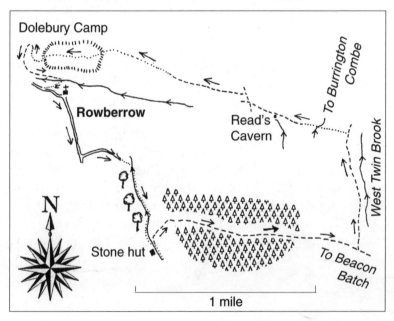

Dolebury Camp

Rowberrow

Read's
Cavern

To Burrington
Combe

West Twin Brook

N

Stone hut

To Beacon
Batch

1 mile

2
ROWBERROW
via Blackdown and Dolebury Camp

This walk leads through a great diversity of scenery; wooded valley, plantation, open moor and limestone upland, with some considerable prehistoric interest. Pub at Rowberrow.

Start:	Rowberrow
Map Reference:	451 583
Distance:	6 miles
Map:	O.S. Explorer 4

In Rowberrow, a small village half a mile north-east of Shipham, park somewhere between the pub and the church – the nearer the church, the less road walking at the end of the walk. Take School Lane, by the pub, and drop into the valley, Rowberrow Bottom. Follow the path upstream past some houses, for a good half mile, until you reach a small stone hut, probably an old keeper's cottage. Here take the track which slopes back up the hill, on your left into the forestry.

Curt notices at every possible deviation will ensure that, so long as you always are climbing, you will not lose the way. To be so commanded and warned, especially in a State Forest, is an offence to any honest British heart, but there is a compensation, that is the great lightening of the spirit when you leave the forestry behind and come into the open hill of Blackdown.

The clear track stretches ahead up the hill; cross the broad grassy gallop, and keep your eyes open for a path leading downhill left. At this point, you may well wish thoroughly to shake off the ill-feeling of the forest on this lovely, breezy upland, and decide to go on to the top, why not? The path is clear and unmistakeable. The summit has been dealt with in another chapter, and needs no repetition. Note well where this descending track leaves; on the west side of a shallow valley with an old fence visible.

Follow the path down West Twin Book till you reach level ground. Here paths come in from the right, and a small detour into the valley takes you to Goatchurch Cavern, some 30 feet above the stream bed on the far slope. Back on the level ground, turn left; presently you will again cross a wide grassy track taking the left of two tracks. Soon, on your right in a hollow, is a good swallet, with a sign 'Drunkard's Pot', and on your left, another, Bos Swallet. Follow the track beside the birch wood a little way, and then it is well worth another detour to see Read's Cavern. Descend left to the stream that flows by the forest edge, and follow the stream down a little way to a twenty-foot outcrop of rock. Here the stream, when full, goes underground and near that, sheltered by the overhang, is the narrow muddy entrance to one of Mendip's several once-inhabited caves, and to my mind, the place where I can most readily picture our ancestors living.

Climb back to the path, and follow on to a crossroads of paths. Here, bear slightly right and uphill, turning left in 50 yards at the National Trust sign 'Dolebury Warren.' Follow the obvious path ahead, through a small plantation, and along the crest of the ridge to Dolebury Fort. This is unusual in that the great banks of limestone rubble do not encircle the summit as is normal in hill-forts, but swoop down the west ridge. Here is a great viewpoint, with Blackdown to the south-east managing to give a greater impression of height and graceful bulk than the map suggests.

Descending through the fortified area, or along the embankments, you will find the exit path at the bottom dropping steeply through ash wood to a lane, where you will turn left to the valley bottom. Walk along the metalled lane by the stream, through a gate for some 300 yards. You will see a fence sloping down the hill on your right; climb the track beside it, which brings you onto a lane, which you follow left and shortly reach the tiled church which is usually locked, and your car.

Among the pines of Rowberrow Forest has been found evidence of a considerable Iron Age iron-working industry.

Read's Cavern

Read's Cavern seems to have been only occupied by Iron Age people, but why them? These were skilled and cultured people whose contemporaries were organised enough to build great hill forts such as Dolebury. Not the sort of folk whom one would expect to be living in a cave without very good reason. Were they perhaps outcasts? The objects found in the caves were largely domestic, the only armament a broken spearhead; they took in bits of a chariot, a pair of fetters, some latch-lifters, and some jewellery. Then one bad day, the roof fell on top of them – you get days like that – and it was not until 1919 that they were discovered.

Dolebury Fort, for all its size, has little to show other than its great defensive banks and superb position, though aerial photographs show traces of contemporary, i.e. Celtic, ploughing. There are some solid square foundations near the apex of the camp which are thought to be of the warrener's cottage, from the days when this was a rabbit warren. Some 'pillow-mounds' – long banks of earth in which the dear little things were encouraged to burrow – can be seen, these could be quite old, any time from the twelfth century onwards.

Rowberrow itself was heavily mined for calamine – zinc carbonate – which was used for the manufacture of brass. It was first discovered here about 1560, and in the early 1700s, produced more calamine than anywhere else in England. About that time, a great deal was exported to Holland, thereafter tending more towards Bristol's great brass-foundries. The residue, and the fumes from the on-site smelting, were rather toxic and had a bad effect on plants and animals, and it has been postulated, to humans too, the calamine-miners of Shipham and Rowberrow and the lead-miners of Mendip being in their day notorious for their wild behaviour, a known result of poisoning.

3
CHEDDAR GORGE
from Black Rock via Beacon Batch and Charterhouse

From the top of Cheddar Gorge, this walk continues some way up the now shallow dry valley leaving it to go by fields towards the highest point of the Mendips. From the airy views of Black Down, descent is made by the Roman settlement to the most interesting area of lead workings, and thence down the lovely valley of Velvet Bottom to the start of the walk. This is a superlative walk, through the very best of Mendip.

Start:	Black Rock Nature Reserve
Map Reference:	481547
Distance:	6.5 miles
Map:	O.S. Explorer 4

The start is at the lay-by where the road up Cheddar Gorge swings right-handed among hazel and ash woods. This is also the car park for the Black Rock Nature Reserve, and particularly during the summer, I recommend that you try for an early start, as this becomes a very busy place. There is nothing to prevent you starting from Charterhouse of course.

Cross the roadside stile, and you will find a signboard which gives details of a short nature trail through the woods on your right. It may be wise to do this interesting detour first, it is well worthwhile, but your enthusiasm may be a little diminished on your return. The trail begins soon after the second stile. To continue, a little further up the clear track you come to Black Rock quarry.

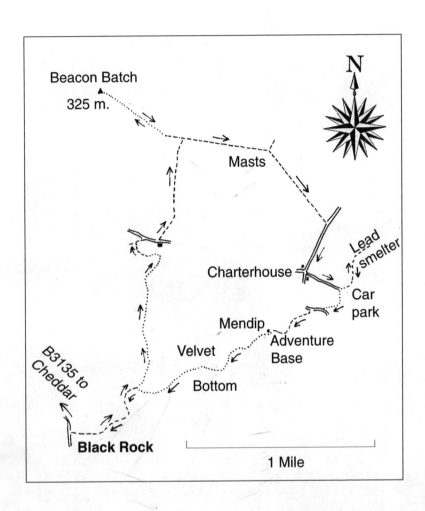

Beacon Batch
325 m.

Masts

N

Charterhouse

Lead smelter

Car park

Mendip
Velvet

Adventure Base

B3135 to Cheddar

Bottom

Black Rock

1 Mile

The strange building set into the hillside is a limekiln, and quite a handsome example. Limestone from the quarry would have been put in at the top of the kiln in alternating layers with coal, or possibly wood or peat, and fired from below. Quite probably a contracting kiln-firer will have done this, as it was recognised as a trade. The result would be lime, which then would most probably be used for spreading on the land to raise the soil alkalinity, or for building, or perhaps limewashing house walls.

From this quarry, continue along the delightful grassy bottom of the dry valley to a step stile near a gate where another valley comes in on your right. Climb the stile, and in the next 40 yards or so, bear left up a shallow defile between thorn trees into a pasture. A gentle slope leads to a gate beside the wood on your left. If is autumn when you do this walk you will assuredly notice the lovely spindle tree with its coral berries by this gate.

Carry on alongside the wood to the next stile. Now the path heads for the top of the thorn hedge on the other side of the field; it would be considerate, and only 50 yards or so further to walk (right-handed) round this field if there is a standing crop. Follow the boundary, losing height, to a slab stile. Aim half right towards a big ash tree, noting the area of 'gruffy ground' on your right, once the scene of opencast mining. Henceforth, the path should head for the left of the white house, but, walking, like politics, being the art of the possible, I suggest you contour to your left for a hundred yards, joining a farm track which leads you down, over a stream, to join a lane. Turn right, and right again on the Shipham-Charterhouse road.

On your left, opposite the white house, is a stile – don't hesitate – climb over it. Now a steady rise alongside the wood, over a stile, and continue alongside the fence; notice the old boundary of thorn trees – they are what gnarled means! Another stile! Up and ever onwards, keenly observing in the stream-bank how you no longer walk on grey limestone, but crunched-up Old Red Sandstone. Just one more stile, to find yourself on a clear, if muddy, track. Here is where the sheep and goats separate; the fainthearted or weary may turn right, to totter desultorily towards the two radio masts; those with high-fibre characters will go left, through the wooden gate to march sturdily up the obvious track which leads to the top, the summit of Black Down, the highest point on the Mendips, 325 metres; 1068 feet.

The triangulation column is set on a tumulus, the only green one among many heather-clad, I wonder why? If the number on the column is not S1516, you're somewhere else. Don't panic, just take the opportunity to think of eight gramophone records ... Oh look, there's Chew Valley Lake, and the Quantocks, the Pen Hill mast – grand views from here. There is heather, and I have seen grouse here.

All about the hill-top are little hillocks a few feet high. These are not baby tumuli, but artefacts of the Second World War, some say decoys – of what I wonder – or devices to make a mess of any enemy gliders that may have tried to land. I like to envisage future archaeologists postulating that Pre-Computer Man's religion was in part to make molehills out of a mountain.

Having sucked your orange, head for the two masts south of you, back along the track you came. At the masts, the track becomes a tarmac road downhill, Rains Batch. On your right is the circular earthwork which has been called a Roman amphitheatre. The OS map coyly describes it as an earthwork, and my own feeling is that it probably was a stockyard; in Roman times, a large population lived here, and needed meat; for handling the animals, a sturdy enclosure between the settlement and the pasture would be necessary. On reaching the main lane, turn right, and then left at the crossroads in 300 yards.

This is Charterhouse; the Roman township was in the field you've just passed on your right, and the Carthusian monks' settlement could have been anywhere, but certainly in the vicinity. You are now back in limestone country, with drystone walls bordering the road. Take a look at the micro-climate such walls create; the sunny side covered with ferns, stonecrop, and many lime-loving plants; the shady side chiefly moss.

Horizontal flues, leadsmelter: Charterhouse

Two hundred yards down this lane brings you to the most absorbing part of the walk. You come to a small car park with an information board, and unless you are in the final stages of exhaustion, I recommend a detour left from here, up the valley to Nether Wood and Blackmoor Pool. There are some very fine flues from the old smelter here, and Blackmoor Pool is a splendid place for frogs and other aquatic wildlife. Return to the car park, and make your way down the valley.

You are surrounded by old workings, some fine 'buddle' pits where once the ore was washed, the water being fed to the pits by leats from the pool. If you're very lucky, you may see adders here – if you do, treat them with respect, and respect their right to be there, please.

Soon you come to a road, which your cross (the children may prefer to go under it through the big culvert), and walk on down the good track on the right bank of the valley, heading west. Velvet Bottom is now a nature reserve and a Site of Special Scientific Interest, and you will be rewarded by reading a leaflet which can be bought from honesty boxes at either end of the reserve. You will soon come to the Mendip Adventure Base, a hut by an unusually tall yew tree. Once again, you find yourself walking on the jet-like slag of yet another smelter, though the remains here are almost obliterated.

Now the valley widens out into a series of long terraces, divided by cross-walls – whether these were fields, or settling-ponds now filled in, I leave you to conjecture upon. At the last of these walls, you will recognise where your are: you've come full circle. All that remains is to retrace your steps of a few very enjoyable hours previously to your starting point.

4
CHEDDAR GORGE
from Black Rock
via West Mendip Way and Cheddar village

This walk begins quietly enough by woods and fields to fine views of the most spectacular inland rock scenery of Southern England from various unusual vantage points; a brief encounter with the frantic human bustle of Cheddar village, especially in summer, provides a nice contrast, the last part of the walk enabling you to recover your contented mien.

Start:	Black Rock Nature Reserve
Map Reference:	481547
Distance:	6 miles
Map:	O.S. Explorer 4

As with the Beacon Batch-Charterhouse walk, you start from the Black Rock Nature Reserve, where the road climbing through the Gorge swings south. Again, I strongly advise an early start if you have a car to park. The first part of the walk, along a good track following the valley is very obvious. At the quarry, notice the angle of the rock strata, sloping from north to south, a pattern you will see repeatedly throughout the walk. Ignore the blandishments of Velvet Bottom which joins on the right after the quarry (what a lovely name, sensuous in an area of rather prosaic placenames); bear leftwards. I do recommend a detour into Long Wood Nature Reserve, it's only going to put a mile on to your walk. The wood is full of interest, not least for

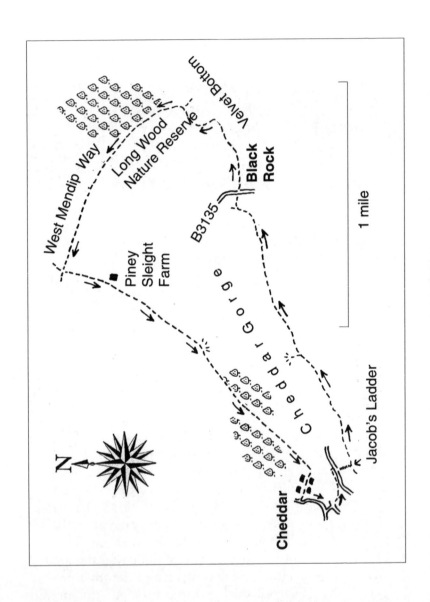

containing Long Wood Swallet, an engulfment cave. The fauna and flora are rich and diverse, and the fossils by the east wall are particularly good. When you come back out of the Reserve, take the path that goes up the west boundary, climbing through an aisle of hazel trees.

Keep to the left of Long Wood Nature Reserve, climbing now up the aisle of hazel trees. Cross the stile, and follow the field edge, by beech and ash and thorn until you reach a farm road. You have been on the West Mendip Way. Now, following the farm road left will bring you to Piney Sleight Farm. The path passes just west of the farmhouse, and so do you, over a wood stile, and across a thin-fleshed field to the gate in the opposite corner. Continue up the next field beside a drystone wall, across another stile and maintain your line to the horizon. Despite sweat and knocking knees, you will not fail to notice the little shallow quarries whence came the stone for the wall. At the top of the slope, make for the flagstone stile with a bar on top.

No, an iron bar – if you have thirst, you've another mile to endure yet. Here is a view worth stopping for: there lie South Wales, the Quantocks, Exmoor on a good day; Brent Knoll, all round south Somerset to the cliffs of Cheddar. It is well worth wandering left to get a better view of the cliffs, always loud with jackdaws and, usually, the strident evidence of mankind. If, however, the Mendip weather does not smile on you, you may only obtain a good view of your boots. I am really taken by the splendid array of anthills here, a sure sign of well-drained ground. I am not alone; rabbits love to sit on them, and green woodpeckers are often to be seen raiding them for lunch.

From the stile you last crossed, make your way directly downhill, keeping the remains of a wall on your left, through thorn scrub and hill pasture, with Axbridge reservoir on your starboard quarter. You will come to a wooden stile; cross it and plunge on down through the woods. Where the track divides at an oak tree, bear right over the old wall, thence on down, ever down. Over another stile, through a handgate. When you reach the native settlement, bear right past some houses to a narrow lane, which you take to the left, downhill of course! At a T-junction, turn left; where this lane bears right, you should go straight on, down a sunken footpath, which brings you to the White Hart. Fleshpots at last! You may safely indulge, all the calorific intake will be used up very soon.

What you do in Cheddar is entirely your business, but sooner or later you must face the grim reality that you have to climb back to your car.

Continue up the White Hart side of the river a little way, then cross to Jacob's Ladder. This is a very long flight of steps which gains you a lot of height very rapidly, to the consternation of your pulse rate. In the tourist season, a small toll is charged for the the dubious privilege of physical exertion, and should you object, or be penniless, the same objective may be reached by turning up the lane to Gough's Garage and left up Lippiatt Lane, thence following the path for the Observation Tower.

From the tower, you climb the very broad clear track which keeps parallel to the great cliffs on your left, but some 50 yards distant. There are many small tracks leading to good viewpoints. When you come opposite the viewpoint you stopped at on the way down, easily recognised by the wall, you are able to attain probably the best perch from which to view the scene. Walk out, with care, on to a promontory of turf and rock – I do advise the use of the backside as a safety measure.

There, far below, is moiling humanity, pickled in noise and carbon monoxide. It is a reflection on our times that once, nearby , with courage, endurance and endeavour, men won riches from pockets of ore underground; now, riches are extracted from the pockets of visitors. Never mind the people, enjoy the jackdaws, the fluted and cascading rocks, the gymnastic whitebeam trees teetering above the abyss.

Cheddar Gorge from the Observation Tower

Having had your fill of a different angle on life, continue to follow the path upward. There are many tracks on the top here; do not veer too far right, it is better to maintain direction towards the wooded valley you see ahead. You will come presently to woodland, and a track which descends steeply through the wood. All at once you debouch beside the road, and with any luck your car will be there awaiting you.

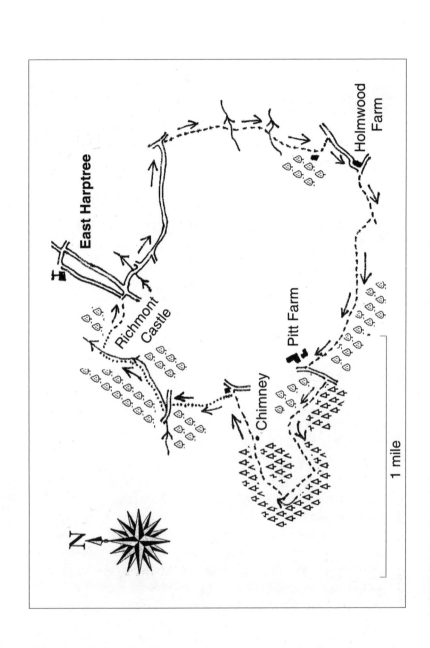

5
EAST HARPTREE
via Richmont Castle

A quiet rural walk in fields, woods, green lanes and a lovely valley, with some relics of old industry and a derelict castle. Pub at East Harptree.

Start:	East Harptree
Map Reference:	565 560
Distance:	5.5 miles
Map:	O.S. Explorer 4

In East Harptree, parking is no problem, somewhere in the back lane above the pub, the Waldegrave Arms. Walk up this lane, bearing left at the top, to cross the 'main' road, and take Culver Lane, below the farm buildings. This is a lovely country lane on which you continue, past Morgan's Lane end, to a T-junction. Here, turn right up a green lane. The big house to your left is Eastwood Manor, of which a little more later. The odd structure on your right is the airshaft of an aqueduct.

Go on to the gate in Arm Covert, then up the next field where the old track is visible as a shelf cutting across the slope. Keeping about 100 yards to the left of the cottage, you will come to an iron gate, whence you drop down to cross a small brook. Now go up the side of the wood, over a barbed-wire fence and over a decrepit iron fence next to a house on your right. You are now on a metalled track; go left, and then right up a narrow, high banked lane. Right and left around the farm buildings, then right, and straight up a rough track, Glendown Batch.

Some 200 yards up the hoof-marked Batch, turn right through a wooden gate opposite an attractively-shaped larch tree. Cross the field to the gate by the water-trough, then slant up the next pasture, aiming at first for the right-hand end of the shelter-belt, then, when you see them, the lower of two gates. Follow the hedge to the next gate, by a row of beech trees, then go along the lane to where it joins the 'main' road above Pitt Farm. Turn left and climb to the Forestry commission entrance to East Harptree woods.

Now you can enjoy easier way-finding for a while, bearing right at all junctions till you reach East Harptree chimney. The chimney is now in sight long before, circling, you reach it, a lot of the wood having been clear-felled and replanted. The chimney was once the top end of the flue which took the fumes from the lead smelting works which are now almost obliterated, there being just a few mounds, and some banks of black, shiny slag visible as you go down the track from the chimney. The pond beside the chimney has much character; a quiet haunt for herons seeking frogs.

Take the path downhill, noticing the slag heaps on your left just before you cross the stile, and go straight down the field and over another stile. Turn left and cross a further stile, across the field to the next stile. Circumvent the large shakehole, dropping down the field to the bottom right corner, where you have to climb two stiles in two yards as you cut through the corner of the wood. A shakehole is an incipient pothole; water has dissolved a shaft in the limestone and the ground has collapsed, creating a crater. Often there is a fissure visible, more frequently a skin of turf covers the cleft, and thus they are always dangerous, you could drop through! Many old mine workings are superficially similar, but they can be recognised by the excavated spoil around them or nearby. Now drop down the steep field to the gate, and turn left along the lane.

After crossing the stream, climb the new stile on the right. Don't follow the rising track, but cut across the grass to a fragile stile into the wood by the stream. Follow the track down through this lovely, jungly wood, ignoring the small sleeper bridge. When at last you come to where a very obvious track crosses the combe, turn right up the reddish earthy slope. Your direction is to keep the fence on your right, but just now, it is time to go back in time, for all these odd mounds and ditches on your left are the remnants of Richmont Castle. When you can bear to leave, you head for the white garage, along the lane which brings you back into East Harptree.

Richmont Castle occupies a steep salient above Harptree Combe. One of the castles erected after the Norman Conquest, its present dereliction gives little indication of its former importance. First owned by one Azeline de Perceval, whose nickname 'The Wolf' suggest

East Harptree chimney

a typical bad baron rather than a Falstaffian, it came under the sway of the de Gourney family later. In the twelfth century, it was felt that women were incapable of being rulers, let alone Prime Minister, and thus came about the civil war when Matilda, Henry I's daughter, was passed over for the succession by the barons, in favour of her cousin Stephen.

Richmont was held for Matilda, and in 1138, Stephen besieged it. After a short while, he made as if to retreat, and the defenders, heedless of what had turned the Battle of Hastings 62 years previously, dashed out to accelerate events. Stephen's cavalry attacked the now lightly garrisoned castle, which succumbed quickly to them.

It remained standing until the era of the overrated Tudors, when its owner, Sir John Newton, at some interval between siring eight sons and twelve daughters, had the building materials taken along the road you earlier walked to build Eastwood Manor. There is some argument as to exactly which house was his manor. An effigy of this philoprogenitive gentleman and his brood may be found in the church, a tribute more perhaps to his wife's fortitude than even her fecundity. Richmont Castle has a very strong feeling of the present past and well rewards a quiet hour's reflection.

6
RODNEY STOKE
via Priddy and Westbury-sub-Mendip

This walk climbs the western scarp of Mendip, traverses the plateau for half the distance, visits the individual village of Priddy, the heart of Mendip, and affords wonderful views across Somerset. All the hard work is in the first mile.

Start:	Rodney Stoke
Map Reference:	487 501
Distance:	7 miles
Maps:	O.S. Explorer 4

In Rodney Stoke, on the A371 Cheddar-Wells road, parking is available down the Wedmore lane, opposite the post office. Cross the main road and take Scadden's Lane, beside the post office. In some 400 yards the lane bifurcates; bear left, and take the track up left behind a house and below a wood. Cross the stile, and climb the long pasture between steep ash woods to the stile and gate at the top of the field. You will probably notice the many well-trodden badgers' paths across your route, and such birds as buzzards and green woodpeckers are likely sights.

Continue climbing the obvious path through the Nature Reserve, which debouches onto short turf and outcropping limestone. Aim for the thorn hedge on the horizon, follow the drystone wall uphill to a slab stile in the cross-wall. You are now on the West Mendip Way. Keeping the wall on your right, another 50 feet of climbing completes the

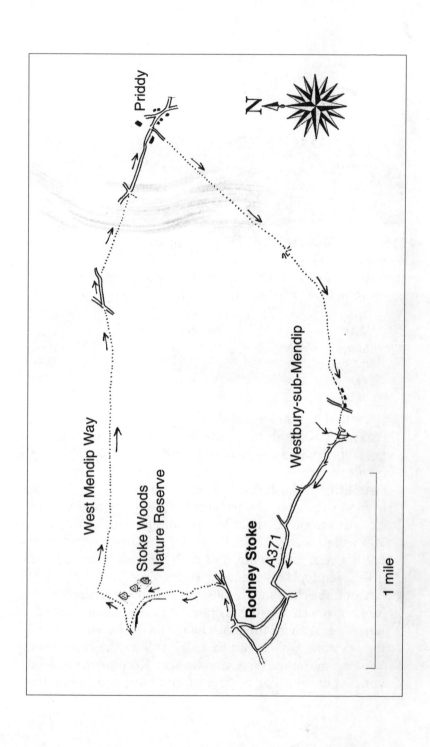

significant height-gain of the walk, and here is a fine place to draw breath and look around.

Follow the wall to a beech-clump, cross a slab stile. Maintaining your direction, you cross another, 100 yards left of the next beech clump. The following stile is some 80 yards left of the field corner; thence head to the left of another beech clump, where the slab stile has been damaged and has some barbed wire entanglement. Now bear slightly right, to follow the wall, through a gate, and the same again to the next gate which opens onto the Westbury-Priddy lane. Follow the metalled lane straight ahead, round the left bend, where you take the gate on the right, and that on the left of it immediately. Walk over the pasture to the stile some way left of the cattle-trough, and bear half-left across the next pasture, which adjoins Coxton End Lane. Join the lane and follow it, not turning left, to Priddy.

A brief dissertation on the village of Priddy and its importance will be found at the end of this chapter, and is best enjoyed over a pint at one of Priddy's two pubs. They lie at the bottom of the green, one on the Wookey Hole road, which you may find more amenable to leg-weary walkers.

As you descend into the village, notice the No Through Road up to your right, the Batch. This is your way: up the lane, through the gate, across the field to the next gate, and the next, straight ahead, near a beech clump with a rookery. Just after this, you will see a declivity on your left, and here, a caving club has been excavating a blocked swallet; worth a look if only to admire the dedication which has driven the cavers to drag out tons of stone and clay in the interests of exploring the dark side of Mendip.

Now aim for the right-hand of two telegraph poles, and cross the slab stile. Head for the slab stile 50 yards to the right of the gate, then towards a pair of thorn bushes, when you see the next stile. Over this, you follow down the right side of the lanky hedge to a wooden handgate at the bottom corner. Here is a splendid viewpoint, ranging from Wiltshire right round via the Quantocks to Wales.

On the hillside about 400 yards south-south-east are the remains of the lost village of Ramspits, among the rough vegetation and thorn bushes. No-one knows just why or when it was deserted, but it is thoroughly rewarding to fossick about the subdued mounds and hollows of the cottages and lanes, to raise the field walls again in the mind's eye, and to people this glorious site which once was home, which saw birth and love, work, laughter and death, and so lives on. I confess to being puzzled at the purpose of the stone-lined declivity in front of the ruined barn nearby; it had something to do with water, I'm sure, but it's perhaps too big for a sheepwash. Such little enigmas are most satisfying – if we knew it all, there would be no room for speculation.

Slant down right to a gate, go on the same slant down the next long pasture. You will see a grey Dutch barn: this is your target. Go through the gate just below it, and follow the metalled lane. Where it joins another lane, cut across below the cultivated ground to a gate, and down to the corner of the lane ahead of you. Turn down left, then right. Here is an atmosphere of content, of warmth and natural prodigality, in great contrast with the spare, lean land you have left above. Some very fine navelwort grows on the walls here, and water springs everywhere.

Walk on up the lane, keeping left where the main lane bears right, and turning down left at the next road, which carries quarry traffic. On reaching the main road, cross it and walk along the lane that slants down. Turn right at the T-junction, and you will soon find yourself reunited with your vehicle.

Priddy Green with thatched hurdle stack

I find Priddy reminds me of Imber, the little village on Salisbury Plain which the Army use for training, and is only accessible at Bank Holidays; there is the same gentle declivity to the village which remains hidden until you are very near, the same feeling of reaching an unsuspected oasis. Priddy makes the most of what little shelter there is from the Mendip winds, and no doubt water was an important factor where surface streams are rare, and springs tend to spring down rather than up! The wide green, round which the village is built, and the five roads converging on it suggest what is in fact correct, that Priddy has long been a meeting point, a focus for trade. A further clue is the picturesque thatched stack of hurdles, used for sheep pens (before the advent of metal pens) at Priddy Fair.

Priddy Fair was started in 1348 during the Black Death when Wells, which had previously been the site, was closed for health reasons. It was primarily the occasion to sell sheep, and woollen goods, but there will assuredly have been dealers, pedlars, tinkers and tradesmen, pickpockets, cut-purses, cheapjacks, fortune-tellers; and an amazing amount of drinking. (The nearest Wednesday to August 21 is Fair Day, even now). In later centuries, miners would buy fresh gear here, and often cattle and horses where traded too.

As well as sheep, the farmers of Priddy will have grown some necessary grain and vegetables, but the end of the eighteenth century saw great changes. This was a period of agricultural revolution, culminating in the Enclosures Acts, and in a few years, the face of Mendip will have altered from being largely sheep-walk to very much its present appearance. The very shape of the fields, the straight walls and hedges, long droves between, tell of organisation; the earlier fields will have been mostly little irregular paddocks. Most of the drystone walls are thus between 150 and 200 years old, and cost about 6p per yard in new money to build. Ploughing became usual, with rotations of grain, roots and grass for hay and grazing. This new kind of farming created more wealth for the farmers, and the workmanlike group of buildings around Manor Farm shows this.

7
PRIDDY PONDS
via Priddy Nine Barrows and Eastwater Cavern

The lead mining industry of Mendip, some of its most notable prehistoric landmarks, and a look at the Mendip underground are the main points of interest on this short but absorbing walk. As the directions are very straightforward, I'll try to explain what you see as we proceed.

Start:	Priddy Ponds
Map Reference:	547 515
Distance:	4 miles
Map:	O.S. Explorer 4

The walk begins at the well-known beauty spot commonly referred to as Priddy Ponds, but more correctly termed Waldegrave Pool. This is on the road between Hunter's Lodge and the Miner's Arms on the B3135; an attractive grove of Scots Pines marks the place. Walk along the dam at the southern side of this large pool, which has in summer dense growth of Water Horsetail. Stepping carefully over the dam sluice, you will soon find a track left which contours round the hillside, in a couple of hundred yards joining a broader causeway coming in from your left.

On the hillside about you are the confusing and indistinct remnants of the Chewton Minery, of which some traces of horizontal flues, and rather more clear signs of the bigger flue rising vertically up the hillside, are all that remain. These flues

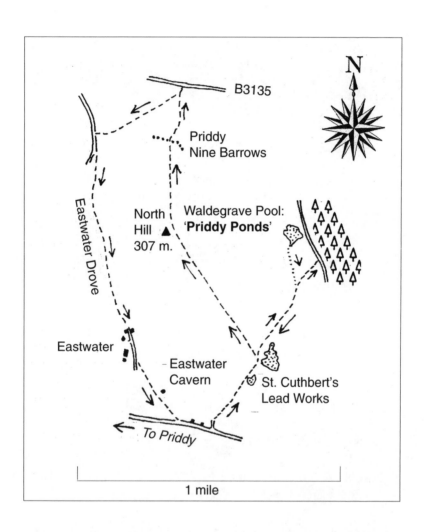

carried the poisonous fumes from the smelting hearths, and served two purposes; the lower parts were almost level and acted as a kind of condenser, much of the lead dust being carried in the smoke settling as it cooled on the inside of the flue, from which it would be collected periodically. Thence, the flue would usually climb away from the works to end in a chimney. Even then they realised that the workers would not live long in dense lead fumes!

Continuing along the causeway, you will notice a lot of the black shiny slag which was left from the smelting process. Soon you reach another pool on your left, whose northern banks boast a good crop of Phragmites Reed, which attracts birds to its rich cover in a sparely-clad landscape. This pond is much deeper than Waldegrave Pool, and at weekends it is common to see wetsuit-clad divers practising and testing their gear. A little way ahead, you will see the complex ruins of St. Cuthbert's Leadworks, but the delights of exploration there must be postponed – you have a little walk to do first!

With your back to the pool, head straight up the hill, following the wall on your left. Cross the fence into a reseeded pasture and continue to the top of the hill by two large round barrows. To your right you will now see Priddy Nine Barrows, which really are rather splendid; there are in fact only eight barrows. Here on North Hill, you stride briefly over the old Red Sandstone, which is confirmation that you are quite high, just over 1,000 feet. You also must stride over a fence which appears to be unblessed with a stile, you should aim for the middle of the row of barrows if you are a purist at following footpaths which are not clear on the ground.

Priddy Nine Barrows: these Bronze Age remains are quietly impressive monuments to whatever our ancestors believed in. Several have been excavated, mostly before the days of exact archaeology, and were found to contain cremated remains, with sometimes grave goods such as beads, which, curiously, came from Egypt. It is all too easy to think scathingly of the chaps who shovelled up these mounds over who knows which chief or king, was this all they could do while Egypt had high civilisation, and the Greeks and Trojans were knocking seven bells out of each other in Asia Minor? These humble humps, were they the best pyramids we could manage? Don't forget, our lads had Stonehenge, for some reason, stone circles all over the place, long barrows, standing stones – they had some very wise and subtle ideas, I'm sure.

The barrows are not pyramid size – probably British understatement, or perhaps the boss was not as vainglorious as a Pharaoh. They left no cities; I wonder if even then city people viewed their country cousins as less bright, cultured and successful? If the barrows were originally conical (having been eroded somewhat in 4,000 years), and perhaps plastered with lime they would have looked quite fine. Still now, they have the power to provoke reverie, indeed reverence.

Back to the present. Strictly speaking, your route heads roughly north to the angle of two shelter belts, then back west-southwest to a gate near the left end of the shelter-belt that the line of barrows point downhill towards. Having reached this gate by fair means or foul, turn left down the lane, and shortly bear left along a 'green' road, Eastwater Drove. This walled trackway gives an enjoyable rural mile to Eastwater Farm. After passing a caving centre, turn left through a gate, opposite the drive to a farm and just before a big farm building on your right. Angle across the pasture towards a declivity, crossing a slab stile on the way.

Eastwater Cavern is a classic cave of engulfment, very similar in the surface features to the famous Gaping Gill in Yorkshire. An ever-deepening valley, dry except in really wet weather, ends abruptly under a small crag. Here is no gigantic chasm, only a cramped hole which leads to a fairly long and interesting cave, which no longer carries the water that first dissolved it into being. Henceforward head towards the road.

On reaching the road, turn left, and then left up a lane just after the third house you pass, a grey rendered building. Walk towards the farm buildings and as the tracks divide, take the middle one over a cattle grid, through a metalled yard in front of yet another caving centre. I recommend this cut through the yard as there is a sign on the obvious road making people like us feel most unwanted – and we don't want to upset anyone. At the other side of the yard you cross a two-bar stile, and another over the Forbidden Road.

Take a little detour here, into the little valley below you, where you will find St. Cuthbert's Swallet. The small stream disappears through a mere crack in the rock, but cavers have made an access hatch by means of a concrete pipe, with a locked hatch. If you feel weary, and long to return to your car as directly as possible, climb back up the path, and follow it among the pine trees to the pool where you started your climb onto North Hill earlier.

However, for the inquisitive, St. Cuthbert's Leadworks stand ruinously opposite you, on the side of the small valley. These were the last lead works to close on Mendip in 1908. Most of the business was in resmelting the slag from previously smelted ore, though some fresh ore came from gruffy ground, i.e. small opencast workings to the east. The ruins are very difficult to decipher, though no mistake can be made about the slag heaps of shiny black detritus, nor of the multiple flues which are quite fun to scramble through. The pools you passed earlier fed water by way of leats to be used for washing ore. This ore washing was one reason, indirectly, for the closure of the lead works; the other main factor being the dramatic fall in the price of lead from abroad. The ore washings went underground, this being Mendip, and trouble arose as these polluted waters emerged at Wookey Hole, where they were the local water supply.

In fact , had there been television in the last century, we may well have watched a saga of unscrupulous lead barons, entitled Priddy.   For, the baddies at Chewton Minery, by monopolising the water at Waldegrave Pool, made life very difficult for those hard working lads at the Priddy Minery, that is where you are now. In 1860, the Priddy boss went to law, and won his case for water. However, he in turn was indicted for water pollution, and lost. This was when St. Cuthbert's took over, under obligations to maintain the purity of water which, of course, was more costly, that cost becoming prohibitive in the end.

Waldegrave Pool, Priddy

When you have explored to your heart's content, you will find no difficulty in returning to where you started your climb of North Hill, and retrace your steps along the old tramway to where your car awaits you.

8
WOOKEY HOLE
via Ebbor Gorge, Pen Hill and Milton

The best way to attain height without the sensation of undue labour is to take an interesting route. This walk leads you from the interesting village of Wookey Hole, tucked snugly under the hill, by way of the lovely, wooded defile of Ebbor Gorge onto the brow of Mendip, where the eye can feast on classic views. A march along a lane precedes a bout of field-walking to Mendip's second highest point, Pen Hill, whence a long and varied descent along lanes and over fields fetches you back to Wookey Hole. Refreshments of all kinds are available in Wookey Hole village.

Start:	Wookey Hole village
Map Reference:	518 458
Distance:	7.5 miles
Map:	O.S. Explorer 4

There is ample parking space in Wookey Hole village. From the river bridge, walk west along a lane between the car park and the cave, past the road-sign 'Unsuitable for Charabancs'. After the last house on the right, Elm Batch, go through the kissing gate and up the field, following the lower, left-hand path. This takes you up a grassy dingle to a wood gate. Go on the clear path some way; when the track divides, your route is to bear right, not up the steep track, but that signed 'To the Gorge'.

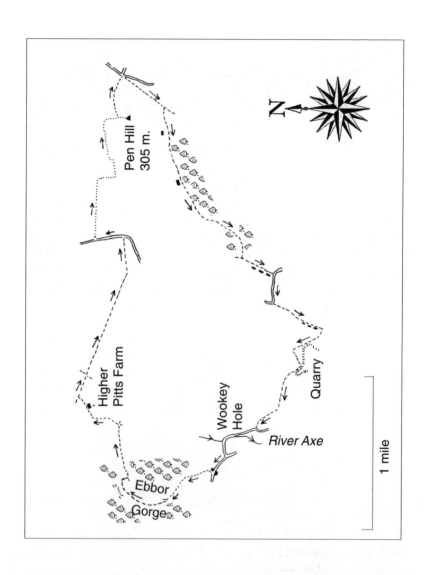

Pen Hill
305 m.

Higher
Pitts Farm

Wookey
Hole

Quarry

River Axe

Ebbor
Gorge

1 mile

Every yard of this is a treat, full of interest to the observant and curious; there are birds to spy in the jungly ashwood, caves to investigate, even a small scramble to enjoy. Ebbor Gorge is not imposing or magnificent, but should you fail to enjoy it, see a doctor at once. At the top of the little scramble, there is a novel view, looking back; a vista is always enhanced by a restricted foreground, it exaggerates slopes, lightens the background and increases the dramatic impact.

Shortly, you reach a T-junction of tracks; turn right up the hill, and then left onto the West Mendip Way, signed Priddy. Soon you cross a stile, and again after a short climb. Following the ruts, with the tall mast on your starboard bow, you come to another stile near a very curly beech tree. Continue up the side of the field to Higher Pitts Farm, where you go through the yard, which can be very muddy, round the back of the farmhouse to the green lane. The dogs here are friendly. On the green lane, turn right and, after a mile or so, you will reach the Priddy road from Wells, by a wood.

Turn left up the road, and pass two gates on your right till you find a stile by which is a post informing you that Pen Hill is a mile distant. It doesn't look so far, but it is. Cross this stile and, following the direction arrows, you will cross a concrete stile, a rail stile and another concrete one, where you turn right up the side of the field, and follow round to another stile on the far side, some 50 yards down from the corner. Walk by the enormous stay of the mast, through the gate, when a slantwise course up the slope will bring you to the lane that the mast engineers use.

Here, at the second highest point on Mendip, is another wonderful viewpoint. No doubt most people feel that to have an enormous metal pipe, 1,000 feet high, sat on this lovely hill is a small price to pay for better TV reception, but then, we live in an age of distorted values.

From this high point, take the tarred lane down to the main road, turn right and immediately take the private road right, and fork right shortly. A pleasant mile and a half later of walking a clear track, you reach a joining of four fields. Here you could have a slight problem, depending on the exigencies of crops, so I shall give the route as an alternative. Ideally, you should turn right, to contour across the field towards a line of trees, where you find a hollow way leading directly down hill, becoming deeper all the time, till you reach a lane at the bottom. Alterna-tively, from the field-junction, head straight downhill and, keeping the wood on your left, follow the field boundary all the way down and round until you reach the hollow way you attain by crossing the fence.

On the lane at the bottom, turn right and walk on to a very sharp right-hand bend, where you go through a handgate on your left, and cross the field to a stile leading into a wood. Follow the path to the next lane, where you turn left downhill, past a number of houses turning right at the bottom. A good metalled lane leads you to the edge of a big quarry on your left; you must follow this quarry round, keeping it on your left. Follow on the track which becomes a lane, and eventually joins the road into Wookey Hole.

Wookey Hole, the cave, paper mill and associated collections are now a major tourist attraction, and well worth a visit. The papermill is especially interesting; and it is instructive to observe how the water of the Axe has been leated to provide energy; study here of an intact system will help you puzzle out some of the derelict mills you come across on your Mendip rambles. It's also worth recalling that the existence of the papermaking industry here contributed to the probably inevitable demise of the lead industry on the hills above.

9
CROSCOMBE
via Ham Woods and Maesbury Camp

This is a delightful rural walk with some variety of terrain, starting from a pleasant, relatively unspoilt village, to climb easily by a wooded valley and quiet fields to the lofty panoramic eminence of an ancient hill fort, thence a long, gentle descent, much of it by a secluded green lane through tranquil countryside back to the start. No great dramatic points, nothing to fizz the blood – simply, a very pleasant walk.

Start:	Croscombe village
Map Reference:	591 444
Distance:	5.5 miles
Map:	O.S. Explorers 4 & 5

In Croscombe, find somewhere to park near the church. From the west end of the Church, climb Church Lane, and turn right. Cross Thrupe Lane at the top of Rock Street, and walk along the lane opposite, by the post box. Go through the iron gate behind a new house. Go on, beside a barbed wire fence, shortly dropping into a small valley. Bear left up this valley to a stile and gate, which leads into the wooded valley of Ham Woods.

These are bonny woods, in the low reaches being mostly ash growing out of limestone scree, and further up the valley being replanted with conifers, beech and larch. There are many badgers living here, a little elementary tracking should lead you to at least one sett; other wildlife abounds,

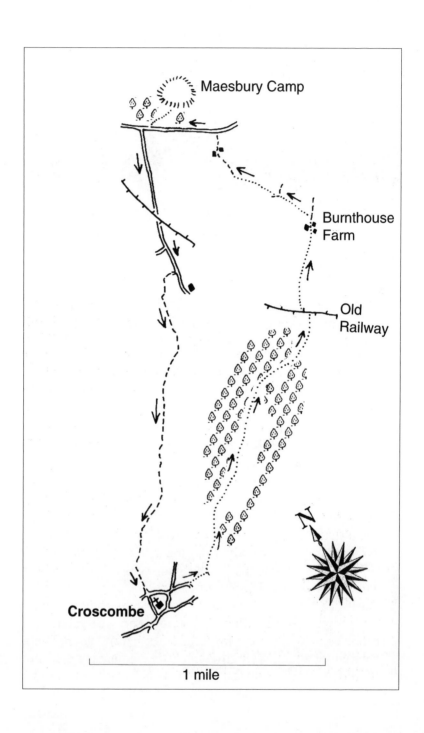

Maesbury Camp

Burnthouse Farm

Old Railway

N

Croscombe

1 mile

particularly roe deer, squirrels, and woodland birds. This is a dry valley, though after rain you could fairly term it muddy. Though you've hardly started walking yet, I do recommend that you sit quietly somewhere in these woods – it's the best way to see wildlife, and there's a lot to be seen here.

After about one and a half miles in the wood, you come to a point where the paths go in various directions. To avoid muddy bits, be prepared to leave the floor of the valley on your left; soon you will see a railway viaduct arching above you to your left. Climb the slope (there is no clear track here) to the left, or west, end of the viaduct, where you will see remains of an old gateway.

Two little puzzles here; among the ballast of the disused railway, most of which is limestone of course, are many nodules of flint. As this was the Somerset and Dorset railway, I wonder whether the flint came from Dorset? The other curiosity is the existence of four gateways in the parapets of the viaduct – gateways that step into fresh air! I am convinced that S and D railway Company weren't making provision for communal suicide, so what are they for? At the end of the walk I shall suggest an answer, which I can't guarantee is right, only possible.

Cross the track of the railway, climb the wooden gate opposite. The way goes across a small field, through the right-hand of two gates. Thence to the next gate, keeping the hedge on your left; then work up left to the farm track which leads you through the yard of the friendly Burnthouse Farm. Having passed through the yard, turn left into the next field, by fuel tanks on baulks, and cross the gate which has a wall on one side and a hedge on the other. This leads into a field with a row of oak trees; you need to exit at the far end of the row.

You now find yourself in a green lane – maintain your

direction into a field, where you make for the gate diagonally opposite, just over a tarred track. Ahead you will see Thrupemarsh Farm, for which you direct your paces to pass between the house and the newly converted farm buildings, then up the metalled track to the road.

On the road, turn left, and walk on, below the golf course, a small wood, ignoring the metalled track there, until about 50 yards before the Dinder road turns left, you climb the stile by the gate on your right, and slant back up the pasture to the top corner of the wood, and through the gate. Now you are at Maesbury Camp.

Maesbury Camp is an Iron Age defensive fort in a fine position, as they usually are. On a good clear day the view from this vantage point is very extensive and memorable. In its day, this was undoubtedly a very important place. It is a little frustrating that so little is really known of these hill forts – their usual purpose, the organisation involved in building them, and not least, how they were defended, with such a long perimeter. Today it is a quiet place, the only screams of frenzy and outrage coming from the adjacent golf course when a member's game is going awry. The Mendip to south coast Roman road passes at Maesbury's northern edge – further evidence to suggest that the Romans developed existing routes, possibly?

Having drunk your fill of scenery and skylarks, and fortified by the knowledge that it's effectively downhill from now on, 700 feet in two miles, return to that same gate where you came in, and down the pasture to the road again. Take the lane down left, signposted Dinder and Croscombe, passing what appears to be the site of a one time army encampment. Where the Dinder road bears right, you bear left and in a couple of hundred yards, turn right up a green lane. A large farm building of delicately-wrought corrugated iron gladdens the eye – you follow the lane round it and try to forget it. There now follows an idyllic mile and a half; this is a green lane that cannot fail to delight as it secretively winds between the fields.

A sense of timelessness comes over me here, it would have been similar for a medieval friar, one of Alfred's soldiers, or a skirmish-weary band of Royalist horsemen. To find quietness is to be free to imagine, and silence, or the absence of artificial noise, is very hard to achieve. When we become truly civilised, there will be at least one day a week when no cars nor planes fly!

As a rule, I am averse to notices that forbid, or claim privacy with threats; along this lane you will see many signs saying No Shooting, No Hunting – I can't say I disliked these! I have often been disconcerted by sudden shots in my vicinity as I've rambled around, and it makes one feel a little unwanted.

Eventually you come to the edge of the Croscombe valley; the track now becomes metalled and drops steeply down between high wooded banks directly to Croscombe.

Croscombe has some very attractive buildings, and several mills by the stream which give an indication of its former importance as a cloth making community. The centre of attraction is the church, which sports a spire, rather an unusual feature in Somerset, far famed for its wonderful church towers. It is so nice to find a church open; and a pleasure to see the wonderful woodwork within. The bulk of it is early Jacobean, the ornate, roofed pulpit being dated 1616; the rood screen is imposing and intricate, all the pews are embellished, and the chancel roof was perfected in 1664.

There is an unusual addition to the church at the back of the south aisle, a two-storeyed chamber which was used not only as treasury and armoury, but the meeting place for the seven Guilds which were once important here and worth recording; The Wives, The Maidens, The Young Men, The

Archers, The Webbers, The Fullers, and The Hogglers (or labourers). Altogether, a fitting place to render thanks for a good walk. Oh yes, the holes in the viaduct – could they have been for shovelling snow through to clear the line? I only ask!

Croscombe

10
STRATTON ON THE FOSSE
via Holcombe and Edford

By lanes and fields, occasionally through woods, this walk takes you from the greatest church on the Mendips to one of the smallest and certainly the best situated, through a Mendip village to follow the remnants of an old canal, and gives some indication of the extent of the old coal mines. There are pubs at Stratton, Holcombe and Edford.

Start:	Stratton on the Fosse village
Map Reference:	659 508
Distance:	5 miles
Map:	O.S. Explorer 5

At Stratton on the Fosse, turn east into the village either by the war memorial or the King's Arms, and find suitable parking, which should pose no problem. Set off past the parish church, an attractive but usually locked building dedicated to St. Vigor – if you've ever met another of that dedication you have now seen the only two. Presently, you turn down the lane to Holcombe, crossing a small valley. Some 200 yards along, a track leads towards fields; you take it, and cross the first field to a stile and gate, then bear right to cross a rail stile into Holcombe Wood.

This wood is a loveliness of daffodils in spring, and later a reek of wild garlic; but regardless of the season, notices scowl at you from every tree it seems, being emphatic as to the

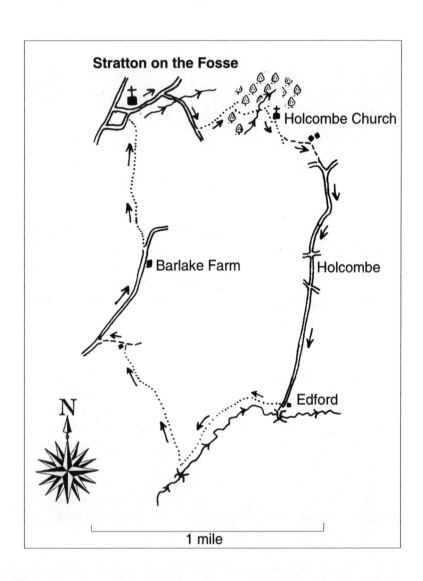

Stratton on the Fosse

Holcombe Church

Barlake Farm

Holcombe

Edford

N

1 mile

privacy of the woods, though grudgingly conceding that you have the right to walk the path you're on. There are even signs proclaiming that mines are set; I cannot decide whether the pin-brains who feel it necessary to guard their pheasants (birds which share the same cranial capacity as those who slaughter them) in this Iron Curtain manner need treatment or derision.

Presently, the path rises, and you climb out of the wood to emerge by the cypresses of Holcombe churchyard.

Where is the village? Ah, well, it used to be in the field above the church, where the humps and hollows of its now grown-over remnants are clear to see; whether the Black Death caused its annihilation, or the edict of some landlord, or the rates were less at the top of the hill, I don't know. The result is that the bonny little grey stone church sits tranquil in the sun, and recalls its gentle centuries serenely. The key may be obtained from the bakery in the village, and reveals an interior unchanged for 150 years at least. Behind the tower is the family grave of Captain Scott's parents, with a special mention for the man himself. This is a very good place to spend the long sleep, undisturbed.

From the church, take the metalled lane that curves up the field, to Moore's Farm, through the farmyard and into the Radstock road. Holcombe shows few signs now of its former status as a colliery village – modern houses are mixed with older houses, some rows of Victorian cottages; a pleasant village though, with a strong community spirit. Your way lies directly through the village, following road signs for Stoke St. Michael and Edford. As you descend the 200 feet towards Edford, you can see the big quarry below Stoke St. Michael, but the general scene is one of woods and fields, an ordinary rural valley. Presently, though, you will observe some indications that other livelihoods than farming have been important here.

As you pass the hamlet of Edford, on your left is a cement works which stands on the site of a fairly large colliery. The difficult state of the roads made the cost of coal from this part of the Somerset Coalfield uncompetitively high, so a canal was proposed to transport the majority of it to Frome, and eventually to Dorset and Wiltshire. Unfortunately the scheme was never completed, so there were hard times here until the latter half of the last century, when the railway came near. Large parts of the canal were dug, however, and as you climb the stile on your right, opposite the large white house just above the Duke of Cumberland pub at Edford Bridge, you will see an obvious canal-style bridge at the far side of the field. On you right, near the road is a short section of dug canal, masonry-lined, and usually containing water.

Walk across to the bridge – after a pint at the Duke? – and cross the stiles to the left of the bridge into the field beyond. Your route goes parallel with the river, a pleasant, chuckling stream. You will assuredly notice the outcrops of shaley coal at the top of the field. The wood across the river is a rare sight in spring, enough daffodils to get Wordsworth going again. Presently, following the field-edge round, you cross a rivulet at a gate, and continue to keep the wood on your left hand. It is disappointing to see that the hillside above has been planted with conifers – I feel they should only be planted en masse where real trees can't grow – and in these fertile valleys, there are many deciduous species that take off very fast.

If you continue alongside the wood, you will arrive at a road-bridge. If you are fired with curiosity and feel you can face a little jungle-busting, you will find a good stretch of the old canal down in the wood; now very overgrown, but with good banks and definite course. In due course, it too leads you to the road-bridge, where perhaps you will parapet-perch, look for fish, and draw breath before regaining the height you lost earlier in the walk.

The way follows the edge of the plantation adjoining the pasture you have just left, past a dump of old iron. The plantation on your left covers the scars of medieval coal pits – they made more disturbance than a lot of later mining, being open pits rather than shafts and adits. Keep climbing by the tiny stream, through a couple of stiles as you come to them, until you arrive at the stupendously incongruous block wall of the garden of a big modern house more notable for its views than its architectural understatement. Notice that the soil in the field to your left is quite black. Bear right round the garden wall of this house, to the field gate, where you turn uphill in the lane. At the top of the lane, turn right along Pitcote Lane, for a pleasant half mile.

After Barlake Farm, go through the next gate on your left. Suddenly the imposing tower of Downside Abbey appears, and the path heads for the gate to the right of the tower. It ostensibly continues across the next field to a stile by a telegraph pole, but, should there be crops growing, it's no great penance to circuit the field left-hand down. The next stile, across a pasture, is also beside a telegraph pole. Once again, the path heads for a gate opposite, but if there's barley or whatever growing, it's little further to cut round the field to your right. This brings you to an obvious tractor-track round the side of the next field to some big farm buildings. Walk past these and you are safely back in Stratton on the Fosse.

The great feature of Stratton is of course Downside Abbey. This is not an ancient place; before 1814 it was a mansion, Mount Pleasant. It was then bought by the Gregorian Benedictines who had earlier fled their seat at Douai due to the French Revolution. The majority of the great church with its pale green copper roofs, visible from afar, is in the high Gothic style, but the place has not yet the feel of generic growth which one associates with older monastic foundations. Perhaps a couple of centuries will grace it with the glow of years and sense of timelessness which characterises old churches. That there is a school intertwined with the Abbey does give the place life and purpose, and whatever one's faith, this great 'wonder of Mendip' at least gives satisfaction to the eye, ear and heart, which cannot be said of, say, the Pen Hill mast or the Whatley quarry.

Holcombe Church

11
CHARLTON
via Beacon Hill and Doulting

A grand stride up the Fosse Way as a green lane, the historic
interest and views of Beacon Hill, a couple of pastoral miles
gently descending to the interesting village of Doulting, after
which some intricate way-finding leads to a straightforward
field walk back to the car. Pubs at Beacon Hill and Doulting.

Start:	Charlton, near Shepton Mallet
Map Reference:	631 432
Distance:	7.5 miles
Map:	O.S. Explorer 5

To begin at the beginning, you must find the old turnpike
house on the A361 Frome road half a mile east of Shepton
Mallet. The house is of the usual triangular form and is
characterised by several large ammonites built into the
walls. Turn down the lane behind the house, and park by
the mill buildings at the bottom, with consideration to
people working there.

The route-finding for over two miles is very simple – walk
up the lane, initially tarmac but soon a green lane, paved
occasionally, a relic of its past as a coach road – hence the
turnpike house. Someone clearly believes it still is a coach
road; some distance up the lane is parked a defunct
twentieth-century one. A mile and a half along, just before
joining a metalled lane, is a small quarry on the right, where
a small badger sett may be found. Turn right on the lane,

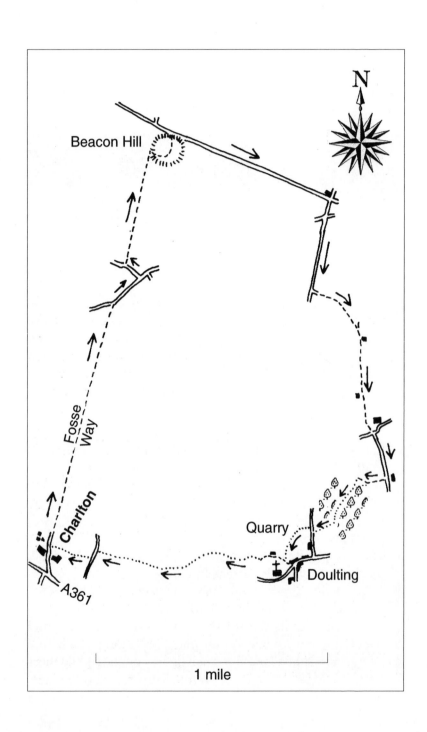

N

Beacon Hill

Fosse
Way

Charlton

A361

Quarry

Doulting

1 mile

and left in 200 yards; the Fosse Way is regained as a beguiling track overhung with bushes, opposite a gate. As you continue northwards, you will notice the pronounced camber or agger, a distinctive feature of Roman roads.

When you reach a plantation of beech, look out for a very fine boundary stone. There is now a short, steep climb to the top of Beacon Hill. Bear right at the top to examine the mounds and earthworks which are plain to see under the large beech trees, as they inhibit undergrowth. This hilltop was once a major crossroads, for here the Roman road from the Mendip lead mines to the south coast crossed the arterial Fosse. The earthworks are not the usual rounded rectangle, however – perhaps the place was important before the Romans came?

Now follow the road right, eastwards, for half a mile, where you will find a pub at a crossroads. As you are nearly halfway … Then turn right, and straight across, down the long straight lane, with such wide verges it must have been a drove road. Turn left in a third of a mile, and follow this lane along to the end, through a gate, across the bottom of an orchard, through another gate, across a paddock to a gate in the corner beside a house; this is indeed the right of way, though you now follow the flagged path from that house to the road.

Now go down the lane ahead to the first house, and cross the wooden stile opposite, and follow the field fence round by a small quarry on the left into the corner by a gate. Go through the gate, and immediately right through a gap in the wall, and walk though the thin wood, keeping just right of the rubbish tip. Very soon you come to the shallow Doulting quarry; you go round it clockwise, over two stiles and over a metal gate to join a lane at the quarry entrance. Go up this lane to the road.

Cross the road and follow the path alongside the field with caravans to a gate by a tin shed. Now turn left to a small gate by tennis courts, and follow below the fence and wall to the corner, where you hop over the wall at a kissing gate. Now down a very narrow alley which lets onto a lane. To visit the church, turn left and right; to see the tithe barn, turn left to the main road and, crossing it, go a short way down the Evercreech lane.

To continue the walk, turn right down the lane, past the wall. Bear down right, passing a water trough which is fed from St. Aldhelm's Well, good water, and bear right by a small waterworks. Follow the path between the pools, noticing the watercress in the rivulet, climb the steps and the stile and turn left. Follow the fence down the field to the gate at the bottom.

Head for the gate that confronts you, then the next, and once more a gateway. Keeping the hedge near on the left, you come to a pair of stiles with a sleeper bridge over a ditch, and straight ahead another arrangement much the same. There is another stile-bridge-stile at the top corner of the next field, whence follow the hedge round right to a grey gate. Cross this, and walk down the short track to a lane. Here, turn left; after a couple of hundred yards, cross the iron stile on your right and, as you cross the field, aim for the two brick mill-chimneys. You will come to a high stone wall, which you walk beside to a stone stile in the corner; now a short path leads you to the Fosse, and your starting-point.

Doulting is far famed for what it stands on – beds of lovely pale limestone, from which material blossomed Wells Cathedral and many other fine buildings in the area. The route of the walk passes several of the old, worked out quarries, and one new, working quarry. This Doulting Stone, like Bath Stone, is a free stone, having no graining, which makes it excellent for carving and intricate work, as is being done now in the restoration of the statuary at Wells. These quarries are small, discreet and somehow fitting – how different from the big business, blast-and- shovel, let's make millions out of

Mendip, roadstone quarries which ulcerate the countryside. There is some relationship between methods and results, I feel; on the one hand, that stone which is won quietly and in proportion to the surroundings is used to make lovely, balanced things; while that which is riven and gnashed from the ground, amid endless dust that whitens the trees and makes porridge of the streams, is largely used to create motorways, more cubic office blocks, more examples of the exquisite beauty of the twentieth century which we take to the paths and woods in an attempt to escape.

Do not miss the glorious tithe barn, which stands a few strides along the Evercreech road, one of the great buildings connected to the Abbey of Glastonbury. Its proportions, stonework, timbering and roof inspire awe, and great pleasure.

Tithe Barn, Doulting.

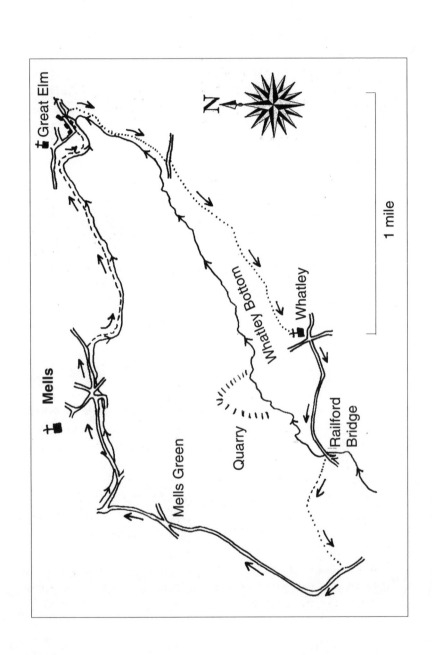

12
MELLS
via Great Elm, Whatley and Mells Green

The first part of this walk is certainly the most interesting, following the Mells River downstream through its deep wooded valley, with all about you indications of the historic importance of the area. From the almost Japanese beauty of Great Elm, your way then proceeds by wood paths and field paths to Whatley, and circumventing an enormous quarry, back via more rural ways to the striking and unusual village of Mells.

Start:	Mells village
Map Reference:	730 490
Distance:	6 miles
Map:	O.S. Explorer 5

Mells has quite a complex of little streets; to park I would recommend one of the quiet lanes down the hill near the river, west of the road to Frome. You need to find the road to Great Elm, which is opposite a most novel triangular bus-shelter. A little way along the Great Elm road is a mounting-block, which was to enable the unathletic, or ladies encumbered with vast skirts, to climb aboard their one-horsepower transport. In about 400 yards, a metalled track turns off right. March gaily along it, beside a river.

You will notice how the comparatively wide valley narrows quickly to create what an optimist might term a gorge. This is encouraging, as gorges very often have interest as well as scenic drama. The steep contours in an otherwise rolling landscape suggested defence to our forebears, and here, your route passes between two great prehistoric forts: Wadbury Camp on your left and, a little farther down, Tedbury Camp on the south side. Also, the river gradients through gorges tend to be steeper, and thus the river lends itself readily to harness as a source of energy. This, too, has happened here. As the track bends eastward, below great overgrown buttresses of Mountain Limestone, you pass the lower sluice of the leat which drove water-wheels up in Mells. Soon, you notice that the pace of the water has slowed, being dammed up by another sluice. Just beyond this sluice, and between your path and the river, is a very large, slightly ruinous building, in front of which is a fascinating and complicated area of industrial remains.

This was one of the famous Fussell's Ironworks, renowned throughout the land for their superb edged tools – scythes, axes, billhooks and so on. Some of these pits would be where hammer mills forged the steel, elsewhere the tools were annealed and honed; at the back are what appears to be hearths or kilns. There is a wonderful feeling of derelict grandeur in this secretive jungly glen, you can sense the ghosts of those men whose hard work and craftsmanship made this part of Somerset a fine example of what industry could be if kept in proportion. The Mells mills were closed about a hundred years ago.

Having walked along behind the buildings, follow the path on down the riverside. The path appears to go through various rock gardens and across lawns, but do not be disturbed, just keep going by the river. You pass a small wood of spruce trees at one point, and some 200 yards downstream of this plantation, the track climbs away from the valley floor, to emerge in Great Elm. Turn downhill right immediately, and you soon find yourself in a lovely part.

Here, the Mells river widens into a broad pool made cheery with ducks, and having an almost oriental air of peaceful, studied beauty, induced by the unusual rustic boathouse. This pool is the result of a mill-dam some way downstream. The last time I was here, I was delighted to see that some lateral thinker was emulating the Canadians by floating his firewood down the river.

Having fed the ducks with those less succulent morsels from your lunch-pack, you climb the hill away from the pool for 100 yards or so, then turn right into the woods. The track initially is deeply rutted by tractors as it contours along the edge of the wood, with fields on your left. Presently the way becomes more congenial, and to your right you can see part of Tedbury Camp on the opposite side of the valley. An enjoyable few hundred yards beings you to the road at Murder Combe.

Turn left for a few yards, then right, keeping the hedge, then fence, on your left for some distance, and then on your right when you arrive at a gate. At the end of this field, you cross the fence into the field on the right, and head on with the rather unattractive solitary rectory on your left. Cross the small field to the church, the churchyard being reached by a stile.

Alas, this is another of the many churches which is locked as a rule, the reason, apparently, to prevent theft from the offertory. It seems a curious attitude to adopt, that the established Christian church, which controls a large part of our heritage and history should lock its doors lest its garments be defiled. I now make a point of commending those churches whose vicars do keep their doors open.

From the churchyard gate, head south and over the crossroads, to head for Chantry. Presently you descend into the valley again, to cross the brook at Railford Bridge. In the woods just upstream was sited another of Fussell's works. Your route crosses the stile on your right, to follow the brook's left bank for a short distance. A streamlet comes in on your left, and you walk up beside it, crossing a stile out of the field.

The steep hillside of boulders and trees above you is largely the unwanted overburden from the gigantic quarry at Whatley. There is a path, indistinct at first, which winds up this little valley to come out into a field at a stile. Here you continue up the slope, keeping the stream and hedge on your left. Straight ahead beings you to a gate into the Chantry-Mells Green lane.

A few minutes walk takes you to Mells Green. Cross the road to descend the unfenced lane past the school. A little short cut, heavily used by schoolchildren, to your right cuts off a corner, to reach the road at the bottom of the valley. Walk downstream, that is, to the right then cross the Mells river, and turn uphill. This pleasant village lane takes you past a number of delightful thatched houses. After some winding about, you join the Frome road by a bus shelter, and turn right. Now on your left is the lovely Mells Manor. This noble house, owned by the Horner family, whose idiosyncratic table manners have contributed via political satire to our nursery rhyme heritage, has been the focus for local Catholicism.

Mells once belonged to the rich demesne of Glastonbury Abbey, but with the Dissolution, the estate was bought by Thomas Horner, whose father John had been bailiff for the Abbey earlier. It was probably a good purchase, as a fair amount of redevelopment had been done under Abbot Selwood; the best portion is the little street that leads to the church. The Manor House was built soon after the estate changed hands, and was in the form H initially, unlike the usual Elizabethan E form. Elizabeth did not sleep here, but Charles I did in 1644. The current Horner was a

Parliamentarian at this time (the Civil War), and was away from home, rebelling, and his estate was sequestered. Is this the cause of the line 'to seek the straw in some sequestered grange' ?

Mells church is very fine though yet again, frequently locked. However, its greatest glory is the tower; no key required, only wonder. It is a masterpiece of buttresses, windows and pinnacles, built sometime in the early 1500s. It is only rivalled by Edward Horner on horseback in the north chapel – one wonders what ecclesiastical reaction would be to such a thing in our enlightened times, when the church officials won't even let you have 'Mum' carved on your mother's headstone.

From the church, walk back along the little medieval street, turn left, and downhill, you soon come to the triangular bus-shelter, and can no doubt remember where you parked your vehicle.

Great Elm

More books from Ex Libris Press:

The essential companion to **MENDIP RAMBLES**:

The **MENDIPS**
by Robin and Romey Williams

'A detailed and comprehensive portrait of the Mendips, which will reward the armchair reader with an insight into all there is to know about this captivating part of Somerset. For those able and willing to walk or drive, this revealing handbook will provide weeks, if not months, of pleasure exploring the scenic and historic landscape, so ably described and photographed.

Written in a clear and flowing style, readers are introduced to the history and prehistory of the Mendips ... Much emphasis is placed on Mendip towns, villages and hamlets, flora and fauna, including local geology and use of land. Even isolated pubs are discussed – just for their historic importance, of course!'

– from a review in *Somerset Magazine*.

176 pages, numerous illustrations; index; Price £7.95

Also available, by the same authors:

The **SOMERSET LEVELS**
*In similar format to **The MENDIPS**, Price also £7.95*

In addition to the above, Ex Libris Press publishes a range of over 50 titles on the West Country and countryside matters generally. Please ask for a full descriptive catalogue. Our books are available through your local bookshop or direct from the publishers:

EX LIBRIS PRESS
1 The Shambles, Bradford on Avon, Wiltshire, BA15 1JS
Phone/ Fax 01225 863595